THE REVOLUTIONARY WAR LIBRARY

What Was the Revolutionary War All About?

JOHN MICKLOS, JR.

Enslow Elementary

an imprint of

Enslow Publishers, Inc.

40 Industrial Road
Box 398
Berkeley Heights, NJ 07922
USA

http://www.enslow.com

Frontispiece: George Washington reviews troops at Valley Forge during the winter of 1777–1778.

Enslow Elementary, an imprint of Enslow Publishers, Inc.

Enslow Elementary® is a registered trademark of of Enslow Publishers, Inc.

Library of Congress Cataloging-in-Publication Data

Micklos, John.
  What was the Revolutionary War all about? / by John Micklos, Jr.
    p. cm. — (The Revolutionary War library)
  Summary: "This book presents a general overview of the causes leading
up to the American Revolution, the war, and drafting the
constitution"—Provided by publisher.
  Includes bibliographical references and index.
  ISBN-13: 978-0-7660-3014-5
  ISBN-10: 0-7660-3014-8
  1. United States—History—Revolution, 1775-1783—Juvenile literature.
  I. Title.
  E208.M46 2008
  973.3—dc22
                          2007024445

Printed in the United States of America.

10 9 8 7 6 5 4 3 2 1

Produced by OTTN Publishing, Stockton, NJ.

To our readers: We have done our best to make sure all Internet Addresses in this book were active and appropriate when we went to press. However, the author and the publisher have no control over and assume no liability for the material available on those Internet sites or on other Web sites they may link to. Any comments or suggestions can be sent by email to comments@enslow.com or to the address on the back cover.

Every effort has been made to locate all copyright holders of material used in this book. If any errors or omissions have occurred, corrections will be made in future editions of this book.

TABLE OF CONTENTS

CHAPTER ONE

A Shot Heard Round the World

The church bell in Lexington, Massachusetts, rang an alarm early on the morning of April 19, 1775. It warned that British soldiers, or regulars, were marching toward the town. Paul Revere and other patriots had ridden through the night to sound the alarm: "Turn out! Turn out! The Regulars are out!"[1]

Soon a small group of armed citizens had gathered on Lexington Green. These were not professional soldiers, like the British regulars. Rather, they were farmers and tradesmen who had joined the local militia unit, pledging to turn out for military service if called upon in an emergency. The militia leader, Captain John Parker, told them to stand ready.

When the British troops arrived, their commander, Major John Pitcairn, ordered the militia to leave. "Throw down your arms! Ye villains. Ye rebels."[2] Greatly outnumbered, the militia slowly began to move away. But then a shot rang out. No one knows who fired it, but more shots

Militia members used weapons like this musket. They carried powder horns to hold gunpowder.

NIGHT RIDER

Before the Revolutionary War, silversmith Paul Revere was best known for his engraving of the Boston Massacre of 1770. Today he is remembered for riding through the night to alert people that British troops were marching toward Lexington. "I alarmed almost every house, till I got to Lexington," he later wrote.[3]

The British captured Revere that evening. One soldier, he later recalled, held a pistol to his head and threatened to "blow my brains out."[4] They later released him.

For many years, few people knew about Revere's ride. In 1863, Henry Wadsworth Longfellow published a poem titled "The Midnight Ride of Paul Revere." That poem made Revere famous.

followed. The skirmish lasted perhaps two minutes. Eight patriots had been killed. Ten more were wounded. A single British soldier was wounded.

The British troops, who were known as redcoats, marched on toward the town of Concord. They hoped to seize guns and supplies hidden there. They also hoped to capture patriot leaders Samuel Adams and John Hancock. The British wanted to stop what they saw as a growing revolt.

At Concord a much larger force of militiamen had gathered. British units clashed with the Massachusetts men at a bridge outside the town. Under deadly gunfire, the redcoats fled. After regrouping, they set off for Boston, where British forces were headquartered. Throughout the long march, they were shot at by militiamen hiding inside houses and behind trees and walls. "We were fired on from all sides," wrote one British soldier.[5]

Militiamen charge retreating British soldiers at the North Bridge, outside Concord.

Years later, poet Ralph Waldo Emerson called the battle at Concord "the shot heard round the world."[6] The day's fighting marked the beginning of the Revolutionary War. But the seeds of the conflict had been growing for decades.

* * * * *

The first permanent English settlement in North America was established in Jamestown, Virginia, in 1607. By 1733, thirteen British colonies stretched from New England

The Pilgrims landed in America in 1620 seeking religious freedom.

Colonists in Jamestown, Virginia, load barrels of tobacco onto a ship. Jamestown was established in 1607.

to Georgia. Many people in the colonies had never seen England. Yet they continued to see themselves as English. They enjoyed the freedoms of English citizens and were protected by British power. They supported the king.

During the 1760s, however, the ties between Britain and its North American colonies started to weaken. Colonists began to think England had an unfair amount of control over them. They believed they were being denied their rights as English citizens.

During the French and Indian War, colonial militias fought alongside British regular soldiers.

Surprisingly, one event that contributed to this belief was a war in which British regular soldiers and American colonists fought side by side against French soldiers and Indians. Among colonists, this struggle for control over North America was called the French and Indian War. The war began in 1754. By 1763, the British side had won. Britain gained control of Canada from France.

But the war led to several problems between Britain and the American colonies. For one thing, King George III issued a proclamation closing land beyond the Appalachian

Mountains to settlers. The Appalachians were on the western frontier of the colonies. The proclamation was an effort to keep peace with the Indians. But many colonists did not like it.

Also, England had gone into debt to pay for the war. British officials believed the colonists should help pay some of the war's costs. Parliament, England's lawmaking body, decided to raise money from the American colonies through various taxes. First Parliament passed the Sugar Act. This law made colonists pay a sum of money for all molasses and sugar brought into the colonies. Then Parliament passed the Stamp Act. It taxed printed material, including books, newspapers, and playing cards.

By the KING,

A PROCLAMATION,

Declaring the Cessation of Arms, as well by Sea as Land, agreed upon between His Majesty, the Most Christian King, and the Catholick King, and enjoining the Observance thereof.

GEORGE R.

WHEREAS Preliminaries for restoring Peace were signed at Fontainebleau, on the Third Day of this Instant November, by the Ministers of Us, the Most Christian King, and the Catholick King: And whereas for the putting an End to the Calamities of War, as soon and as far as may be possible, it has been agreed between Us, His Most Christian Majesty, and His Catholick Majesty, as follows; that is to say,

That as soon as the Preliminaries shall be signed and ratified, all Hostilities should cease at Sea and at Land.

And to prevent all Occasions of Complaints and Disputes which might arise upon account of Ships, Merchandizes, and other Effects, which might be taken at Sea; it has been also mutually agreed, That the Ships, Merchandizes, and Effects, which should be taken in the Channel, and in the North Seas, after the Space of Twelve Days, to be computed from the Ratification of the present Preliminary Articles; and that all Ships, Merchandizes, and Effects, which should be taken after Six Weeks from the said Ratification, beyond the Channel, the British Seas, and the North Seas, as far as the Canary Islands inclusively, whether in the Ocean, or Mediterranean; and for the Space of Three Months, from the said Canary Islands to the Equinoctial Line or Equator; and for the Space of Six Months, beyond the said Equinoctial Line or Equator, and in all other Places of the World, without any Exception, or other more particular I stinction of Time or Place, should be restored on both sides.

And whereas the Ratifications of the said Preliminary Articles, in due Form, were exchanged at Versailles, by the Plenipotentiaries of Us, of the Most Christian King, and of the Catholick King, on the Twenty second of this Instant November, from which Day the several Terms above-mentioned of Twelve Days, of Six Weeks, of Three Months, and of Six Months, for the Restitution of all Ships, Merchandizes, and other Effects, taken at Sea, are to be computed.

We have thought fit, by and with the Advice of Our Privy Council, to notify the same to all Our loving Subjects; and We do declare, That Our Royal Will and Pleasure is, and We do hereby strictly Charge and Command all Our Officers, both at Sea and Land, and all other Our Subjects whatsoever, to forbear all Acts of Hostility, either by Sea or Land, against His Most Christian Majesty, and His Catholick Majesty, Their Vassals, or Subjects, from and after the respective Times above-mentioned, and under the Penalty of incurring Our highest Displeasure.

Given at Our Court at Saint James's, the Twenty fixth Day of November, in the Third Year of Our Reign, and in the Year of Our Lord 1762.

God save the King.

LONDON:

Printed by Mark Baskett, Printer to the King's most Excellent Majesty; and by the Assigns of Robert Baskett. 1762.

Colonists welcomed the end of the French and Indian War. But many of them disliked King George's Proclamation of 1763.

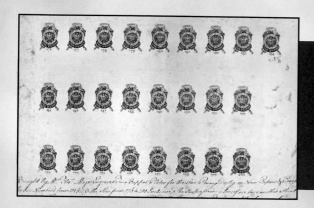

Under the Stamp Act of 1765, all books, newspapers, and other items printed in the colonies had to carry a tax stamp like the ones pictured here.

The colonists were not allowed to vote for members of Parliament. This meant they had no say in how they were taxed. Many believed this was unfair. "No taxation without representation" became a popular phrase.[7] Soon colonists set up a boycott. They refused to buy many English goods.

In October of 1765, delegates (representatives) from nine colonies met at the Stamp Act Congress in New York City. They said that Parliament had no right to tax the colonies. But the

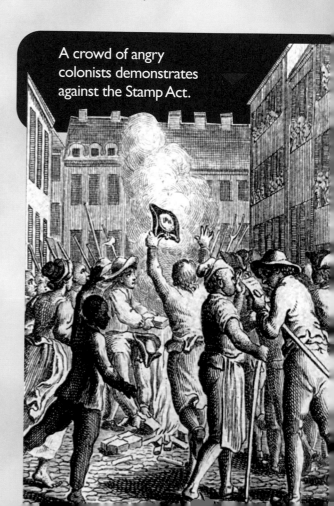

A crowd of angry colonists demonstrates against the Stamp Act.

BOSTON MASSACRE

On March 5, 1770, a crowd gathered near the Customs House in Boston. They threw icy snowballs at the British sentries on duty. "You dare not fire," they taunted the soldiers.[8] Then someone in the mob threw a club. It knocked down Private Hugh Montgomery. Getting up, the British soldier leveled his musket and fired. Soon more shots echoed in the night.

When it was over, five colonists were dead. Six others were wounded.

actions of ordinary people had a much greater impact. Colonists rioted. They attacked tax collectors.

The protests worked. The taxes were repealed, or canceled. Soon, however, Parliament set up new taxes.

Many colonists were angry that there were British troops in America. On March 5, 1770, that anger led to deadly violence in Boston. Yet even this event, known as the Boston Massacre, did not lead to war. Five more years would pass before the "shot heard round the world" was fired.

CHAPTER TWO

The War Begins

On December 16, 1773, an Indian war cry rang out in Boston. A group of Massachusetts patriots pretending to be Mohawk Indians rushed to the wharf and boarded three ships loaded with British tea. They dumped 342 cases of tea into the harbor. Colonists called this the Boston Tea Party. The lost tea was worth $90,000, a huge sum at a time when the average worker earned less than a dollar a day.[1]

King George III believed that "there must always be [at least] one tax" on the colonies.[2] This would show that England had the right to tax colonists. By 1773, the only British tax the American colonists paid was on tea. And in spite of the tax, English tea was cheap.

Still, colonists thought the tax was unfair. They decided to boycott English tea. The Boston Tea Party took matters even further.

When news of the dumped tea reached England, King George was outraged. He encouraged Parliament to pass laws called the Coercive Acts. These acts aimed to coerce, or force, the people of Boston into changing their

Britain's King George III believed that he had the right to tax the American colonists.

behavior. The British banned town meetings in Massachusetts. They closed the port of Boston. They also sent more soldiers to the city, and colonists had to allow these soldiers to live in their homes. The colonists believed these measures violated their rights as British subjects. They called them the Intolerable Acts. Intolerable means unbearable or impossible to accept.

In September of 1774, more than fifty delegates from the colonies met in Philadelphia to discuss what to do. This meeting was called the First Continental Congress. The delegates issued a declaration of American rights. It called on Parliament to repeal the Intolerable Acts. To put pressure on Parliament, the colonies agreed to stop importing or using any goods from Great Britain.

But the delegates to the First Continental Congress made clear that they still considered themselves "his majesty's most loyal subjects."[3] Like most Americans at this time, the majority of delegates wanted to mend ties with England.

For his part, King George seemed eager to put the rebellious colonists in their place. "Blows must decide whether they are to be subject to this country or independent,"[4] he wrote in November of 1774.

Meanwhile, everyone waited to see what would happen in Boston. Tensions mounted. Then came the battles at Lexington and Concord in April of 1775. War had begun.

Soon more than 10,000 American militiamen from throughout New England took up positions outside Boston. They kept the British troops bottled up in the city. That was not too difficult. Boston lay at the end of a peninsula. It was connected to the mainland by a narrow

Patrick Henry of Virginia (opposite page) argued for American independence. But other delegates to the First Continental Congress (right) were not ready to break with Great Britain.

strip of land. The redcoats did not dare try to march across that narrow land.

But when the Americans built dirt walls on a hill on nearby Charlestown Peninsula, the British had to do something. From Breed's Hill, the Americans could fire cannons at Boston. So on June 17, British troops tried to

SIZING UP THE WAR

BRITISH ADVANTAGES

- England had the largest navy in the world. At the start of the war, the thirteen colonies had no navy at all.

- The British army had well-trained troops and seasoned generals. The British also hired thousands of German professional soldiers. The Continental Army had little battle experience.

- Many American colonists supported the British.

AMERICAN ADVANTAGES

- It took months to travel by ship from the colonies to England and back. This made it difficult for British leaders to respond to developments in America.

- The Americans fought with passion because they fought for freedom and to protect their land.

- The Americans received support from Britain's enemies, such as France.

The determined Americans made the British pay a high price to capture Breed's Hill. More than a thousand redcoats were killed or wounded.

storm the hill. "Don't fire until you see the whites of their eyes!" the American troops under the command of General Israel Putnam and Colonel William Prescott were ordered.[5] American gunfire turned back two British attacks. Finally, the British took Breed's Hill and nearby Bunker Hill. But more than a thousand British soldiers were killed or wounded in the

This painting shows George Washington taking command of the Continental Army in July of 1775.

fight, which came to be known as the Battle of Bunker Hill.

Just days before the battle, the Second Continental Congress had created an official army. It was called the Continental Army. Congress chose George Washington of Virginia to lead it. He had fought in the French and Indian War. General Washington took charge of the army at

Cambridge, Massachusetts, in early July of 1775.

Many members of Congress still hoped for peace. In early July, Congress sent the Olive Branch Petition to King George III. The king turned down this appeal to restore good relations with the American colonies.

Many British generals had considered the American rebels an "untrained rabble" they could easily defeat.[6] By the end of 1775, however, some had begun to realize they were in for a long fight.

The Olive Branch Petition was a last attempt by colonial leaders to resolve disagreements with Great Britain.

CHAPTER THREE

A Daring Declaration

After nearly a year of war, many colonists still hoped to mend ties with England. Then, early in 1776, a writer named Thomas Paine published a pamphlet called *Common Sense*. It called for independence. England had rejected "every quiet method for peace," Paine said, so "for God's sake, let us come to a final separation."[1] In less than three months, 120,000 copies of *Common Sense* were sold. More and more people began to support the cause of American independence.

In July, the Second Continental Congress prepared a document that made the point even clearer. Thomas Jefferson drafted the document—the Declaration of Independence. "All men are created equal" and have certain rights that can never be taken away, the Declaration stated.[2] These rights include "Life, Liberty, and the pursuit of Happiness."[3] If a government destroys or even fails to protect these rights—as Great Britain had, according to the

Thomas Paine's pamphlet *Common Sense* (above, right) was extremely popular. It led many Americans to decide to fight for independence.

Thomas Jefferson was the main author of
the Declaration of Independence.

Declaration—the people may set
up a new government.

After much debate, twelve
colonies voted for independence on
July 2. (New York officially voted for
independence two weeks later.) Delegates
formally adopted the Declaration of Independence on
July 4, 1776.

Now there was no going back. The colonies
had officially cut ties with Great Britain. They had
proclaimed themselves "free and independent
states"—the United States of America.[4]

But declaring independence was
one thing. Beating the enemy on the
battlefield would be harder.
Although the Continental
Army had succeeded

in forcing the British out of Boston in March 1776, the Americans lacked organization, supplies, and training. Many Continental soldiers signed up for just a few months. When their time was up, they simply went home.

During the summer of 1776, General Washington was trying to defend New York from a much larger British force. When the British attacked on Long Island, the Americans were quickly beaten. Washington's army was nearly trapped, but managed to escape across the East River. However, the Continental Army was defeated and forced to retreat again. By fall, the British had captured New York City.

Washington knew that the Americans could not win the war in one big battle. But they could lose it that way. He aimed to keep the war going by never risking his whole army. He hoped the British would eventually grow tired of fighting.

John Adams of Massachusetts helped convince delegates to the Second Continental Congress to vote for independence.

25

That outcome seemed hard to imagine in the final weeks of 1776. Throughout November and early December, the British chased Washington's retreating troops across New Jersey. Finally, the Americans crossed the Delaware River into Pennsylvania.

Although they were safe for the time being, the American troops were very discouraged. They had suffered one defeat after another. Many of the troops were due to go

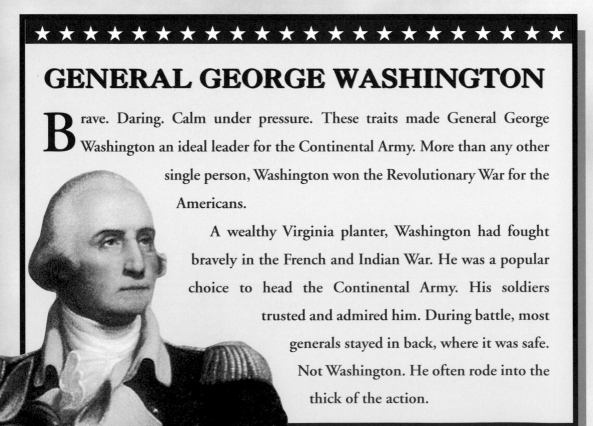

GENERAL GEORGE WASHINGTON

Brave. Daring. Calm under pressure. These traits made General George Washington an ideal leader for the Continental Army. More than any other single person, Washington won the Revolutionary War for the Americans.

A wealthy Virginia planter, Washington had fought bravely in the French and Indian War. He was a popular choice to head the Continental Army. His soldiers trusted and admired him. During battle, most generals stayed in back, where it was safe. Not Washington. He often rode into the thick of the action.

Washington was defeated on Long Island, across the East River from New York City. But his army managed to escape with most of its cannons and supplies on the night of August 29, 1776.

home at the end of the year. No wonder Thomas Paine wrote, "These are the times that try men's souls."[5]

On Christmas night, Washington led his troops back across the Delaware River into New Jersey. After all the soldiers had crossed the river, they began a grueling march to Trenton. Many of the men did not have coats or decent shoes. Major James Wilkinson wrote that the ground

★★★★★★★★★★★★★★★★★★★★★★

CHOOSING SIDES

Not everyone in America supported the cause of independence. Many people believed America should keep its ties to England because the British Empire had helped the colonies grow and prosper. Others did not really care one way or the other. They simply wanted to live in peace. Many slaves joined the British army. The British promised them freedom for doing so.

The people who supported the British were called *loyalists* or *Tories*. The people who supported independence called themselves *patriots*. The British referred to them as *rebels*.

"was tinged here and there with blood from the feet of the men who wore broken shoes."[6]

Around 8 A.M., Washington's army reached Trenton. The town was occupied by a group of German professional soldiers the British had hired. The Americans caught these men, who were called Hessians, by surprise. After a brief but fierce fight, the Hessians surrendered.

The Americans killed or captured more than 900 Hessians in the battle. Washington did not lose a single man.

The victory raised the morale of the American troops. Washington decided to strike again. On January 3, 1777, he defeated the British at Princeton, New Jersey.

The battles of Trenton and Princeton helped turn the tide of the war. They made Americans believe they could win.

After American troops crossed the icy Delaware River, they surprised and defeated the enemy soldiers at Trenton.

CHAPTER FOUR

The War Drags On

In June of 1777, the British general John Burgoyne invaded New York from Canada. He commanded an army of more than 7,000 soldiers. His plan was to march south to Albany. There he would link up with

British forces moving north along the Hudson River. This would cut off New England from the other states. It might mean the end of the rebellion.

But Burgoyne's invasion did not go as planned. Supplies ran low. A series of battles wore the British army down. The redcoat force Burgoyne expected to meet him never arrived. By October, Burgoyne was outnumbered and trapped. On October 17, he surrendered to the American general Horatio Gates at Saratoga, New York.

General Burgoyne's surrender at Saratoga was the first time the Continental Army had defeated a large British force. It helped convince France to enter the war on the American side.

This was a major turning point in the war. A large British force had been defeated. And France became convinced that America could win the war. Soon King Louis XVI decided to join the fight against England, the longtime enemy of France. The French had a strong navy. They could provide money, arms, soldiers, and supplies.

But not all the news was good for the patriots. In August of 1777, a British fleet sailed up the Chesapeake Bay. About 15,000 troops under the command of General William Howe landed at Head of Elk, Maryland. Howe began marching his army toward Philadelphia. George Washington quickly moved more than 12,000 men to block Howe's advance.

On September 11, the British and Continental armies fought each other along a creek about 30 miles southwest of Philadelphia. At the Battle of Brandywine, the Americans were defeated. Washington still told Congress that he would "take every

The Marquis de Lafayette, a French nobleman, became one of Washington's most trusted officers.

THE PHILADELPHIA CAMPAIGN, 1777

PENNSYLVANIA

Morristown
American winter quarters
Jan.–May 1777

Valley Forge
American winter quarters
1777–78

Germantown
October 1777

NJ

Brandywine Creek
September 1777

Philadelphia
captured by British
under Howe,
Sept. 26, 1777

MD

ATLANTIC
OCEAN

DE

Chesapeake Bay

VA

Howe, 1777

Delaware R.

| 0 | 50 | 100 Miles |
| 0 | 50 | 100 Kilometers |

→ American troop movement
→ British troop movement
✳ Battle

measure in my power to defend" Philadelphia.[1] But Howe

could not be stopped. On September 26, the British marched

into the rebel capital. Congress had fled the city a week earlier.

The British army spent the winter in comfortable

quarters in and around Philadelphia. Washington set up

camp at Valley Forge. His men huddled in makeshift huts. Many did not have warm clothes. Some did not even have shoes. Food was scarce. During the harsh winter of 1777–1778, as many as 2,500 American soldiers died at Valley Forge. That was about one in four men in Washington's army. Despite the hardships, the Continental Army became a much better fighting force during the winter at Valley Forge.

In June of 1778, the British decided to abandon Philadelphia. They were worried about being trapped in the city if French forces arrived to aid the Americans. The British marched back to New York.

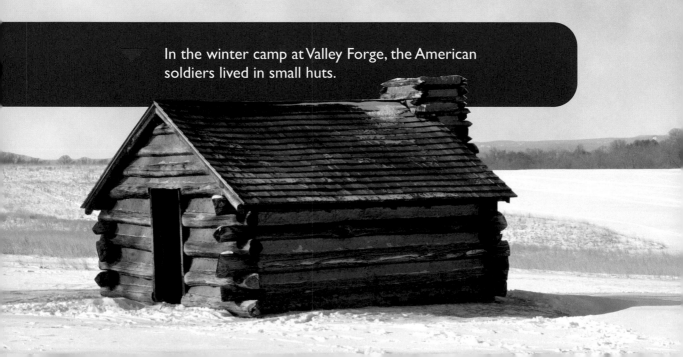

In the winter camp at Valley Forge, the American soldiers lived in small huts.

JOURNEY OF THE LIBERTY BELL

To many patriots, the Liberty Bell in Philadelphia served as a symbol of the Revolution. The bell had been rung in July of 1776 to announce the Declaration of Independence. As British troops approached Philadelphia in late 1777, the patriots vowed to keep it safe. They carefully packed the bell. Then they shipped it in an army baggage train to Allentown, Pennsylvania. There they hid it in a church basement. The bell was returned to Philadelphia on June 27, 1778.

On July 9, 1778, a French fleet did arrive to help the Americans. But this did not quickly change the situation.

The war dragged on. This created problems for both sides. The British struggled to maintain support for the war at home. The Americans had trouble finding money to pay for the war effort. Which side would crack first?

CHAPTER FIVE

Victory and Freedom

During the first years of the Revolutionary War, most of the fighting took place in the North. The British won most of the battles. They also captured the major cities of New York and

Philadelphia. But they were unable to stamp out the rebellion.

British general Henry Clinton decided to try a new strategy. The British would invade the southern colonies. Clinton knew that many people there were still loyal to the king. He hoped these loyalists would join the fight against the American rebels.

In December of 1779, Clinton set sail from New York City with about 8,500 British troops. By May of 1780, these troops had captured Charleston, South Carolina. About 5,000 Continental soldiers and patriot militiamen were taken prisoner. After this, bands of South Carolina loyalists began attacking their patriot neighbors. Patriots struck back. The fighting was savage.

★ ★ ★ ★ ★ ★ ★ ★ ★ ★ ★ ★ ★ ★ ★ ★ ★ ★ ★ ★

CASUALTIES

During the Revolutionary War, about 200,000 men served in either the Continental Army or a state militia for some period of time. It is estimated that at least 6,284 died in battle, and about 18,500 more died of disease.[1]

Clinton's strategy seemed to be working. He decided to return to New York. He left General Charles Cornwallis in charge in the South. In August of 1780, Cornwallis won a big victory at Camden, South Carolina.

Now the only resistance to the British in South Carolina came from a few small patriot militias. These groups struck quickly and without warning. Then they disappeared into nearby woods or swamps. Leaders such as South Carolina's Francis Marion were good at this type of warfare. The British could never catch Marion. They nicknamed him "the Swamp Fox."[2]

In December of 1780, a new American general took over in the South. Nathanael Greene did not have many men. But he

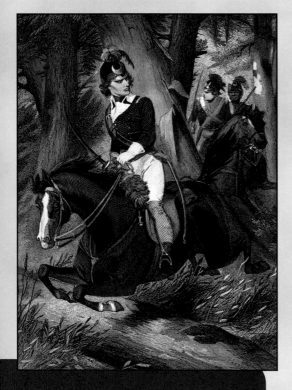

Francis Marion led an American militia in South Carolina. His men conducted hit-and-run raids against the British.

General Nathanael Greene helped defeat the British in the South.

had a plan. He would get Cornwallis to chase him through the rugged countryside of North Carolina. This would tire out the British soldiers.

Greene's plan worked. After two months, the redcoats were exhausted. Greene decided to fight them at Guilford Courthouse, North Carolina. On March 15, 1781, Cornwallis lost more than one-quarter of his men in the battle there.

Cornwallis knew he could not hold North and South Carolina now. He decided to march into Virginia. Eventually, he moved his troops to Yorktown on the coast. That proved to be a mistake. George Washington had joined his army with French forces led by General Rochambeau. In late August, the American and French troops began a fast, six-week march from New York to Yorktown. They hoped to trap Cornwallis.

In the meantime, a French fleet under Admiral de Grasse arrived at the mouth of the Chesapeake Bay. Cornwallis now had no way to escape.

In late September, the American and French forces began attacking Yorktown. Day after day, they bombarded the British with cannon fire. Finally, on October 19, 1781, Cornwallis surrendered his entire army of more than 8,000 men.

It took a month for the news to reach England. At first, King George wanted to keep fighting. But Parliament would not support the war any longer. Yorktown would be the last major battle of the Revolutionary War.

Nearly two years passed before the war officially ended. Finally, on September 3, 1783, the Treaty of Paris was signed. England recognized the independence of the United States.

But the new nation struggled. The government was weak. The states did not always work together.

In 1787, delegates from all of the states except Rhode Island met in Philadelphia. They hoped to solve these

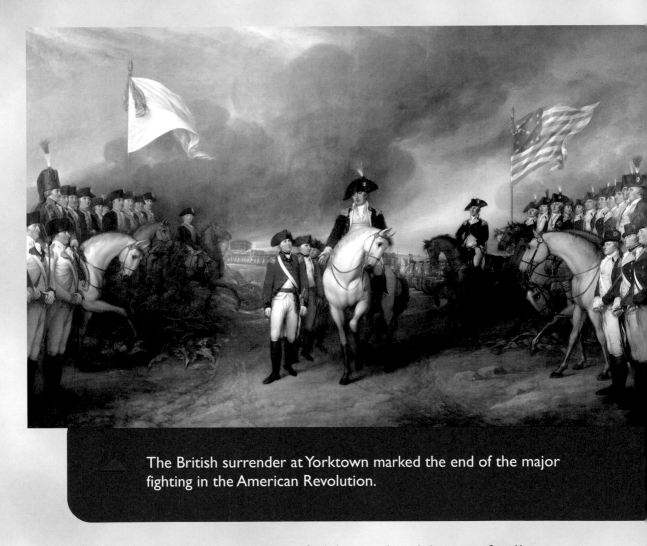

The British surrender at Yorktown marked the end of the major fighting in the American Revolution.

problems. After months of debate, the delegates finally wrote the United States Constitution. The Constitution accomplished what the delegates hoped. It created a government that has helped the United States stay free and strong for more than 220 years.

REVOLUTIONARY WAR
TIMELINE

The Sugar Act of 1764 places a tax on molasses and sugar. Many colonists boycott English products in protest.

The Stamp Act is passed in 1765. In response, colonists call the Stamp Act Congress.

On April 19, Lexington and Concord mark the first battles of the Revolutionary War.

Battle at Lexington

The Continental Congress adopts the Declaration of Independence on July 4.

On January 3, Washington defeats the British at Princeton, New Jersey.

The British defeat Washington's troops at the Battle of Brandywine on September 11.

On September 26, the British march into Philadelphia.

1764–1773   1775   1776   1777

On March 5, 1770, five Americans are killed in the Boston Massacre.

On December 16, 1773, patriots throw crates of tea into Boston Harbor.

The Boston Tea Party

On June 17, the British win a costly battle at Breed's Hill and Bunker Hill.

George Washington takes command of the Continental Army at Cambridge, Massachusetts, in early July.

George Washington captures the Hessian outpost at Trenton, New Jersey, on December 26.

Battle at Trenton

The British general John Burgoyne surrenders his army at Saratoga, New York, on October 17.

Surrender at Saratoga

In December, Washington's troops arrive at Valley Forge for the winter.

John Paul Jones

In September, John Paul Jones wins a sea battle off the coast of England. He becomes the patriots' first naval hero.

On May 12, the British capture Charleston, South Carolina.

On August 16, the British smash the Continental Army in the South at the Battle of Camden, South Carolina.

Battle of Camden

On March 15, 1781, the Battle of Guilford Courthouse in North Carolina cripples the army of General Cornwallis.

Charles, Lord Cornwallis

Cornwallis surrenders at Yorktown, Virginia, on October 19, 1781.

In February, France becomes the first official ally of the Americans.

| 1778 | 1779 | 1780 | 1781–1783 |

American and British troops battle at Monmouth Court House, New Jersey, on June 28. The last major battle in the North ends in a draw.

In December, the British capture Savannah, Georgia.

In September and October, a patriot effort to recapture Savannah fails.

Francis Marion

Francis Marion leads a small patriot militia in attacks against the British army and their loyalist supporters.

On September 3, 1783, the Treaty of Paris is signed, officially ending the war.

Treaty of Paris

The British recognize American independence.

CHAPTER 1: A SHOT HEARD ROUND THE WORLD

1. William H. Hallahan, *The Day the American Revolution Began: 19 April 1775* (New York: William Morrow, 2000), p. 23.

2. Ibid., p. 30.

3. Documents of the American Revolution: Letter from Paul Revere to Dr. Jeremy Belknap, <http://www.historycentral.com/Revolt/battleaccounts/lexington.html> (August 19, 2006).

4. Ibid.

5. Documents of the American Revolution: A British Account of Concord Bridge, <http://www.historycentral.com/Revolt/battleaccounts/lexington3.html> (January 3, 2007).

6. Ralph Waldo Emerson, "Concord Hymn, Sung at the Completion of the Battle Monument, July 4, 1837," <http://www.bartleby.com/42/768.html> (January 3, 2007).

7. John Ferling, *A Leap in the Dark: The Struggle to Create the American Republic* (New York: Oxford University Press, 2003), p. 42.

8. The Freedom Trail: Site of the Boston Massacre, <http://www.thefreedomtrail.org/visitor/boston-massacre.html> (November 27, 2007).

CHAPTER 2: THE WAR BEGINS

1. Alan Axelrod, *The Complete Idiot's Guide to the American Revolution* (New York: Alpha Books/Penguin, 2000), p. 92.

2. John M. Thompson, *The Revolutionary War* (Washington, DC: National Geographic Society, 2004), p. 18.

3. The Avalon Project at Yale Law School, "The Articles of Association; October 20, 1774" <http://www.yale.edu/lawweb/avalon/contcong/10-20-74.htm> (January 15, 2007).

4. Thomas Fleming, *Liberty! The American Revolution* (New York: Viking, 1997), p. 88.

5. Axelrod, p. 128.

6. Gordon S. Wood, *The American Revolution* (New York: Modern Library/Random House, 2002), p. 54.

CHAPTER 3: A DARING DECLARATION

1. Thomas Paine, *Common Sense*, <http://www.ushistory.org/Paine/commonsense/singlehtml.htm> (January 8, 2007).

2. U.S. Declaration of Independence.

3. Ibid.

4. Ibid.

5. Thomas Fleming, *Liberty! The American Revolution* (New York: Viking, 1997), p. 214.

6. David Hackett Fischer, *Washington's Crossing* (New York: Oxford University Press, 2004), p. 210.

CHAPTER 4: THE WAR DRAGS ON

1. John Buchanan, *The Road to Valley Forge: How Washington Built the Army That Won the Revolution* (New York: John Wiley & Sons, 2004), p. 252.

CHAPTER 5: VICTORY AND FREEDOM

1. Thomas Fleming, *Liberty! The American Revolution* (New York: Viking, 1997), p. 334.

2. Ronald W. McGranahan, The American Revolution Home Page, "Brigadier General Francis Marion: 'The Swamp Fox,'" <http://www.americanrevwar.homestead.com/files/MARION.HTM> (August 21, 2006).

boycott—To refuse to buy or use a product, often as a form of protest.

coerce—To make someone do something by force or the threat of force.

constitution—A document creating a government. The U.S. Constitution outlines the government's powers and lists some of the people's rights.

declaration—A formal statement. The Declaration of Independence announced America's break from England.

Hessians—German professional soldiers hired by the British.

intolerable—Impossible to accept or bear.

loyalist—An American who supported the British during the Revolutionary War.

massacre—The act of killing a number of people, especially when they are helpless or not resisting.

militia—Citizens who train as soldiers from time to time and are available to serve in an emergency.

patriots—Americans who supported independence from Great Britain.

Parliament—The legislative, or lawmaking, body of Great Britain.

petition—A formal written request.

proclamation—An official public announcement.

redcoat—A British soldier.

repeal—To withdraw or cancel a law.

representation—In government, the practice of having members of an assembly or lawmaking body act on behalf of other citizens.

Tories—Americans who supported the British during the Revolutionary War.

BOOKS

Cheney, Lynne. *When Washington Crossed the Delaware: A Wintertime Primer for Young Patriots.* New York: Simon & Schuster, 2004.

Maestro, Betsy, and Giulio Maestro. *Liberty or Death: The American Revolution, 1763–1783.* New York: HarperCollins, 2005.

Murray, Stuart. *American Revolution.* New York: DK Publishing, 2002.

INTERNET ADDRESSES

America's Story from America's Library

Jump Back in Time: Revolutionary Period

    http://www.americaslibrary.gov/cgi-bin/page.cgi/jb/revolut

The Declaration of Independence

    http://www.ushistory.org/declaration/document/index.htm

Revolutionary War

    http://www.historycentral.com/Revolt/